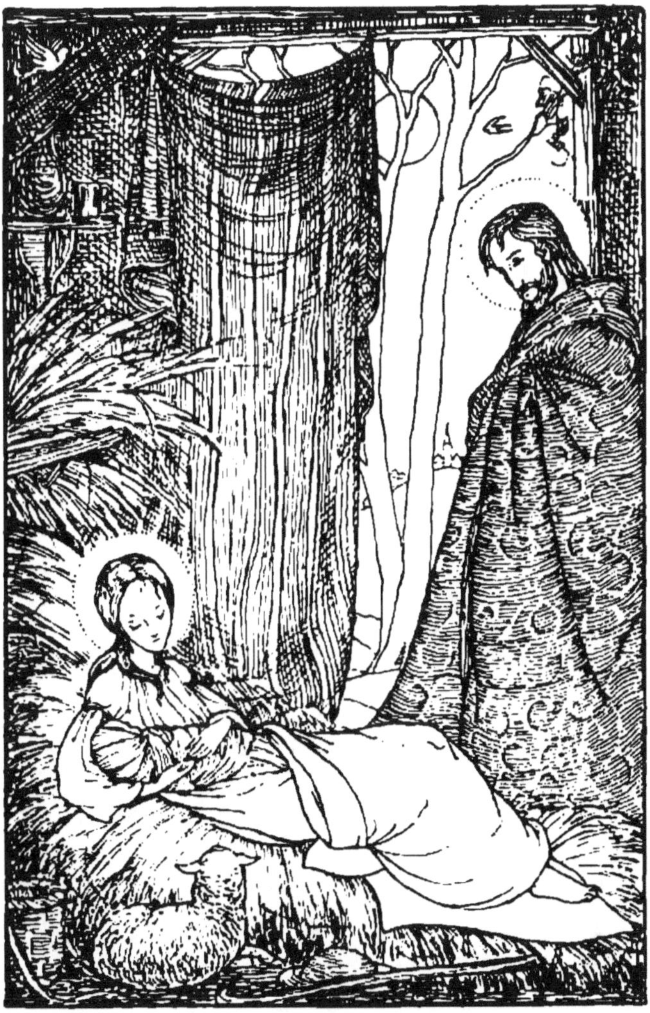

The Nativity

JESUS AND I

*Conversations between Jesus and any child
who wants to talk to Him*

BY

JEAN PLAQUEVENT

Translated by

EMMA CRAUFURD

Illustrations by

MARY TAYLOR

Nihil Obstat: Ernestus C. Messenger, Ph.D.
Censor Deputatus

Imprimatur: E. Morrogh Bernard
Vic. Gen.

Westmonasterii, Die 26a Septembris, 1949

PART I

FIRST CONVERSATION:
MOSTLY ABOUT HOW VERY NICE JESUS IS

You: Jesus, I don't know you very well yet, but I should like to. I know that you are very kind and gentle and that when you smile at people who are unhappy it makes them feel better at once. I know you are never cross with people who are trying to please you.

And I know I ought to love you because you died on a cross for me. If I look at a crucifix for long it makes me want to cry. Those nails must have hurt so and that horrid crown of thorns round your head. I do love you because of that, Jesus, but it is all rather frightening, and if you don't mind I would rather talk to you like you were when you were just the same age as I am. I mean when you were Our Lady's little boy at Nazareth. If I can get to know you when you were a child like me, then we can grow up together.

I think that would be the very nicest way to know you—always the same age as me, until we are both grown up.

So I will talk to you as I would talk to any boy who came into our house to play with me, and you will let me play with you, and will not mind. I am sure children who play with you never need to be smacked or scolded for what they do!

Now, you talk to me, Jesus, so I can begin to get to know all about you.

Jesus: I shall love to be friends with you. I know you very well already, and I am very glad that you want to know me, too. But I must tell you that nobody in the whole world knows *all* about me, not even the Pope. Because, although I am a boy, no bigger than you are, I am also God and no one can know quite all about God. But I can tell you a lot of things.

First of all, it was I who made the sky and the earth and everything you see about you. I made the sea, and the sands beside the sea, for paddling and building sand-castles. And I made the great ocean for ships to sail on, and I put all the fishes in it—little fish and big fish, shrimps and whales, I made them all, and gave them the sea to swim in. I made the great rivers, too, and the little streams, and the flowers that grow on their banks. I made forget-me-nots and daisies and wild roses and buttercups, and all the other flowers you like to pick.

I made the huge mountains and the pine forests that grow on them, and the birds and the little furry animals that live in them. Squirrels and foxes and rabbits, I made them all. I made the warm summer weather, and the frost and snow you love so in winter. I made the sun to give light by day, and I made the quiet night for people to sleep in. I made the rain and the wild wind as well as the sunlight. I made everything in the whole world. In the towns people have rather spoilt the nice green world I made for them, but anywhere in the country you can go out of doors and say, " This is the lovely world Jesus made for us to be happy in, because he loves us."

Best of all, I made you, and I sent you to your mummy and daddy so that they should be happy because they had you, and you would be happy because you had them. I very much want everybody in the world to be happy; and if they do as I ask them, so they will be. And in heaven they will be happier still.

You: But, Jesus, if you made everything, and me too, you must be much too strong and clever to play with me. I wouldn't dare ask you to.

Jesus: I shall be very disappointed if you don't. You see, I made myself into a real baby and grew up to be a little boy, specially so nobody would be frightened of me ever, and so that I could be friends with all the children in the world who want to be friends with me. You will let me talk to you and play with you, won't you? It is so very disappointing when children begin to be friends with me and then forget all about me again.

SECOND CONVERSATION:
ABOUT WHEN JESUS WAS A BABY

Jesus: Before I came to be my dear mother's little son at Nazareth people used to look up and say, " Can it be really true that there is a God who minds what happens to us? Is He really there, up beyond the sky? Yes or no? Is it really true? " You see, they couldn't see me then, and it was very difficult for them to love me or even believe in me. So I came down from heaven and came to be Our Lady's baby and grew up among ordinary people. And I never told them who I was until they knew me too well and were too fond of me to be afraid when they found out that their friend, Jesus of Nazareth, was really God. Since then nobody need say, " Is it really true? " because I came and showed them it *was* really true. The pity is, there are still people who have never heard anything about me. You must be sure to tell them, if you should meet any.

You remember the crib you saw in church last Christmas? There I was, lying in the manger with my mother on one side of me and St. Joseph on the other, and the ox and the ass lying on the straw behind them. That is just how it was on the first Christmas night. My mother and St. Joseph had made a long journey to Bethlehem and when they got there they found there was no room for them in the hotel. So they had to go to a stable for shelter, and that was where they were when I came down from heaven to them as Our Lady's new baby. Perhaps St. Joseph could have found a better place if he had been rich, but he was not at all rich.

Do you remember, too, the Three Kings you saw in the crib soon after Christmas? Those were three kings who had heard of me and who came to see me and love me and give me presents. But on their way they went to see Herod, the king of the country where I was born, to ask him how to find me. They didn't know that he was the wickedest king in the world! They said to him, " Where is the baby who is born to be King? " Herod thought perhaps they meant that this baby would take his crown away from him presently, and he was very angry and very frightened and sent his soldiers to kill all the boy babies in Bethlehem. He thought he would be sure to catch me that way. But an angel came and warned St. Joseph in time for him to get us all away before the soldiers arrived. He took my mother and me and our little donkey and we went and hid in the next country to mine—

a country called Egypt. Herod couldn't find us there.

We had to travel all the way with only the little donkey to help us along, and soon we were all as tired as he was.

When Herod died we came home to Nazareth. There St. Joseph had a carpenter's shop. He made ploughs and cart-wheels and all the kind of things that carpenters still make now.

You: Doors and cupboards and tables and chairs and shelves to put things on?

Jesus: Yes, all those things. And as soon as I was big enough he began to teach me to make them, too. But when I was the size we are now I just used to get the chips and shavings to play with. They were lovely to play with. But St. Joseph had to work very hard all the time to earn enough for us to

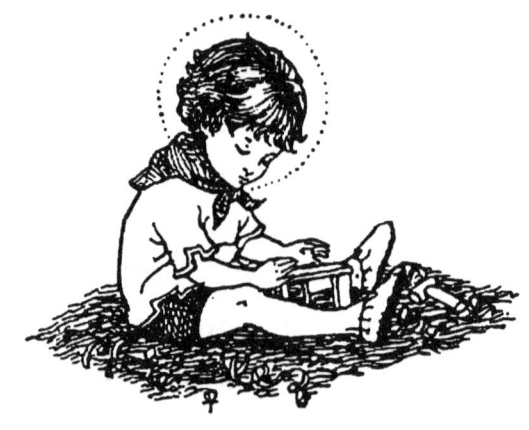

7

pay the rent and the taxes, and to buy food and clothes to wear and all the things that people needed then, just as they do now. My mother had to work hard, too. She did all the housework and all the cooking and all the mending, and she made my clothes and mended them, and looked after the garden and the hens. And she did everything so very, very well. No one ever had such a darling, clever mother as I had—not even you. But all darling mothers are a little like her, and all children are a little like me and think their own mother the very nicest in the whole world!

What I liked best of all when I was very little was to go to sleep in her arms in the evening, listening to her singing, and being so very, very glad I had made her to be my mother and that I had come from heaven to be her little son.

THIRD CONVERSATION:

ABOUT BEING POOR OR RICH

You: I think going to sleep in your mother's arms must feel very nice when you are a baby.

Jesus: Yes, it's the very nicest way to go to sleep so long as you are little enough to fit into them and not too heavy. We should both be much too big, the size we are now! But I want you to understand that I had none of the things rich children have—no expensive toys, nor a big nursery nor a nanny to pick things up after me. We were all very happy at Nazareth, but we were very poor! If you are poor, too, you can be glad we are the same sort of children. If you are rich you must remember carefully always to be as nice as ever you can to children who are poorer than you, because I was one of those poor children myself. I was luckier than some you may have seen, whose clothes are all in rags and who look dirty and as if nobody loved them, but only because my mother and St. Joseph were so good at managing always to have just enough. My mother was specially good at it. She was always mending my clothes and washing them, and she could make wonderful meals with really very little to cook with. When you see any very poor children, ask her to help their mother to manage better; if you feel very poor yourself, ask her to help

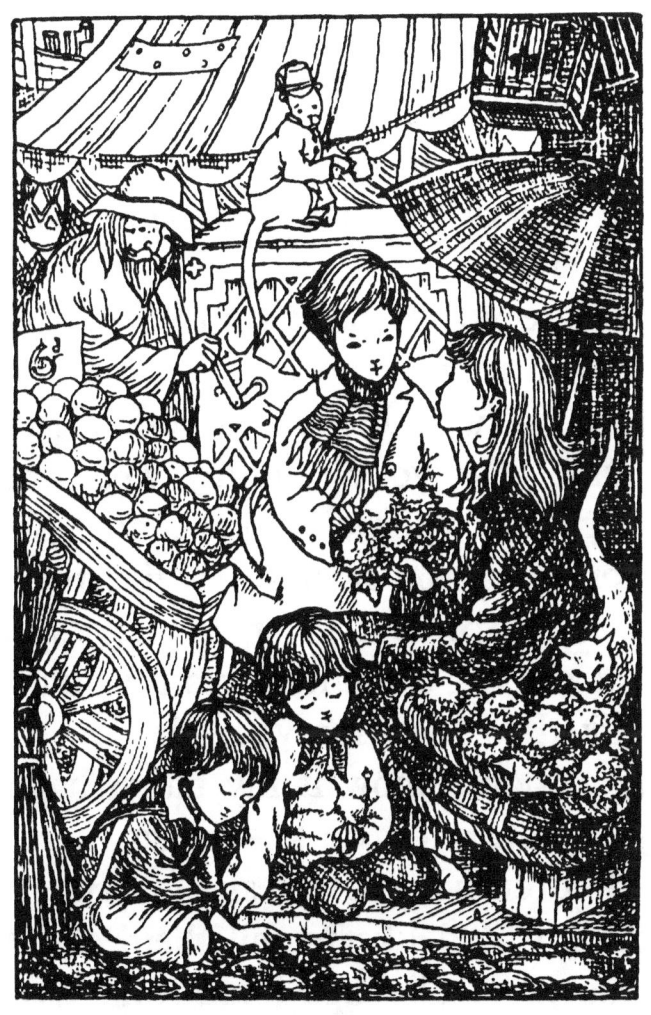

In the Market-place

your mother. She knows just how to do it, and she simply loves to be asked to help mothers who have too much to do and not enough time or money to do it with. You see, she is very proud of having managed so well herself.

If you are not so poor yourself and do not know any children who are, you may be sure there are plenty of them in other parts of the world. Ask your mummy what you can send them; she will help you. And I promise that everything you manage to give them will be just like a present given to me, especially if it should be something you would have rather liked to keep for yourself!

You: I don't know if my father has much money or not, but I do know that there are a lot of children who have less nice things than I have. I would like to tell them about you being poor, too. Perhaps I can some day, but, anyhow, I shall ask Mummy what I can give them and how to do it. I shall like to do that very much, specially now I know it is really like giving presents to you.

FOURTH CONVERSATION:
ABOUT BEING KIND

Jesus: If you remember all your life long that I was poor and that to give things to people who need them more than you do is the same as giving presents to me, we shall always be friends. And I will tell you something else. If everyone in the world were friends with each other and with me, then this world would be very nearly like Paradise— the great garden I made at the beginning of everything for Adam and Eve to live in. Every time a child says he will be friends

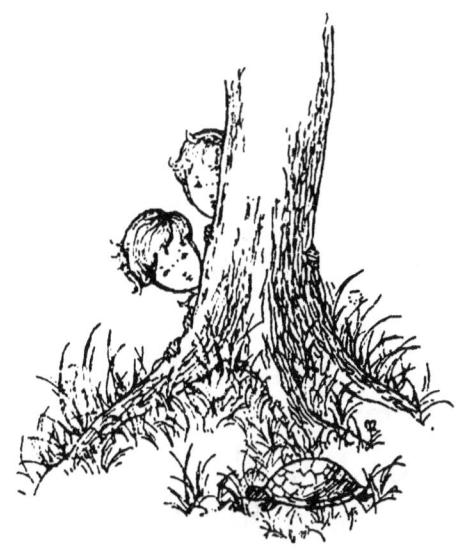

Being Friends

with me all his life, and really means it, the world grows just a little more like that than it was before.

I try so hard all the time to make everybody in the world happy and ready for heaven, and you can help me—yes, you can, even while you are small as we are now. No one is too small to be kind.

You: Who am I to be kind to?

Jesus: Why, everybody! Everybody you ever see, but especially the ones you see most of the time.

Your father works hard, doesn't he? He is busy all day doing difficult and tiresome things so that he will be able to give you and your mother and your brothers and sisters a happy home and food to eat and clothes to wear. Those things don't grow on trees, you know; they have to be worked for. Are you always as nice to him as ever you can be?

Then there is your mother, who works so hard to keep your house clean and neat, who cooks your meals and mends your clothes. Do you try to help her like I used to help my mother?

Then there are your brothers and sisters and the other children you play with—sometimes they are cross, and sometimes you want to be cross with them. But how you would miss them if they were not there and you had to play by yourself all day!

Then there are the people who come to see your mother. She is so proud of you and always hopes you will be very nice to them—I hope you are.

If you always try to be nice to all these people then we shall be great friends, but it isn't always easy, is it?

You: It's very difficult always to be nice, but quite easy sometimes.

Jesus: The more times you manage to be nice when you don't want to, the more like me you will grow, and the happier you will be yourself.

You: Is being nice just the same as being kind?

Jesus: Either means behaving as much like me as you can.

You: When I am cross with Mummy I am always sorry almost at once. The most troublesome thing is visitors, who jump at me and kiss me when I come into the room. I do hate that, and I don't see why they do it.

Jesus: You know, I hated that, too! But the people who do it *mean* to be nice, and I am sure your mummy looks at you just as mine did at me, hoping so hard you will manage not to pull away and make a face. You can manage not to, as I did, if you really try.

You: All right, Jesus, I'll try, and if I even manage some of the times it will be better than not trying at all, won't it ?

Jesus: Much better. And remember, if you ask me I will always come and help you.

FIFTH CONVERSATION:
WHO JESUS PLAYED WITH

You: You know, Jesus, I like you better than I ever did now I know you didn't like visitors who made a fuss of you, and doing dishes and tiresome things like that. I never thought about you having to do all the tiresome things I have to do. But did you play games like I do, too?

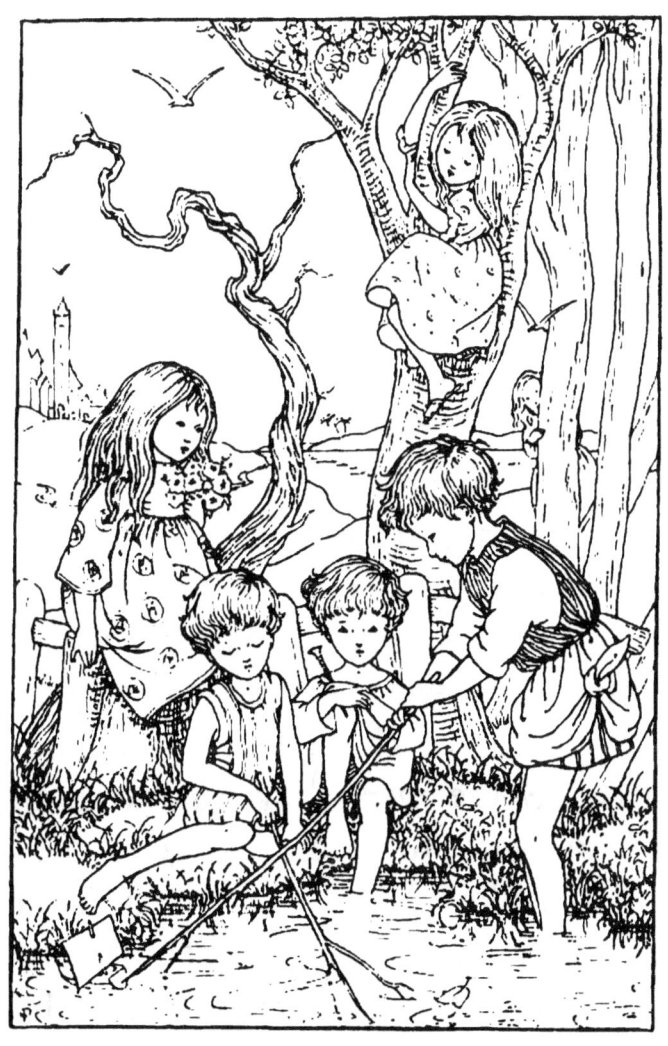

Playing in Nazareth

Jesus: We played wonderful games in Nazareth. There were woods for a game like hide and seek we used to play, only we called it David and Saul. And there was a stream to wade in and sail boats on, and sometimes we went to the big lake of Genesareth, like a sea, with fishermen's boats pulled up beside it. I loved the lake and so did the other children, and our favourite thing was to be taken for a sail by the fishermen. Oh yes, we had quite as much fun as you do.

You: What were the other children like?

Jesus: Like the ones you know. Some were good and some were naughty nearly all the time, but most of them were good and bad by turns. Some were lazy and some always seemed to want to quarrel, and some were rough and rude. But I always knew, and so are you to know, that any of them might grow up to be good friends of mine. The hardest ones to be nice to were the ones who pretended to be very good indeed when really they were not good at all, but mean and nasty. But remember, I could see into their hearts and knew what they were really like. *You* can't do that, and children who seem horrid to you may really be trying quite hard to be good. There is only one child you know all about, so that you can be quite sure whether he is trying to be nice or not.

You: Who?

Jesus: Your own self, of course! You know if you are being good or bad, and so do the other children know about themselves. So if you see another child being naughty, remember, you have often been naughty, too, and say to yourself, " Perhaps he is really trying to be good, but that time it was too difficult. Perhaps he will manage to be good next time." If you always hope people are meaning to be friends of mine, and treat them as if they were my friends already, that is the very best thing you can do for them, and the way I treat them, too.

You: Did you have any special friends, Jesus?

Jesus: Yes, my cousin John, who is called John the Baptist, because after he grew up he baptised so many people. He was nearly the same age as me. I used sometimes to go and stay with him and his mother and father, up in the hills. We used to go exploring, and we caught grasshoppers to bring home (only they generally used to get away before we got there), and we used to find birds' nests, too, and to lie quite still and watch little foxes come out of their holes. We saw a mother fox once, with six cubs all playing round her like kittens. And there were rabbits there, too, and all kinds of little hill flowers to pick and bring home to John's mother.

You: Jesus, I do wish I had lived near your home when you were little. I believe it would have been quite easy to be good if I had had you to play with every day. Nothing would seem dull and a nuisance if you were there.

Jesus: The children I played with did not know me as well as you do. You know I am God, and they didn't know I was anything more than just another boy. And some of them grew up to hate me and to wish for my death. You would not like to have been one of those, would you? But as it is, we can be friends for always; even after the time comes for you to leave this world, we can go on being friends in heaven.

PART II

SIXTH CONVERSATION:

ABOUT THE FIRST DISOBEDIENCE OF ALL

You: Jesus, I have been sent up to lie on my bed and rest, and I don't want to at all; but if I must rest, can we have a talk to pass the time?

Jesus: I will come and sit on the end of your bed and then we can talk comfortably. And I'll tell you something! You very nearly said, " I won't! " when your mummy told you to go and lie down, but you remembered about being nice just in time, and said " All right, Mummy " instead. And do you know, your mummy was so pleased, she said thank you to me, and your guardian angel is smiling all over his face, and I like you even better than I did before.

You: Well, it was worth being good, if it made all that difference. But, oh, Jesus, I do get told to do so many things in a day, it's very difficult always to do them!

Jesus: I'll tell you a story about the very beginning of everything. When we, the Holy Trinity—that's God the Father, God the Holy Ghost, and I—first made the angels, we asked them to do something for us in return for being made so great and strong and shining and beautiful. Most of them agreed, but the grandest angel of all said, " No! I am as great as you are! " And he went among the other angels, saying, " Just turn your backs on God and then you won't be bothered by Him. As soon as you can't see Him you will be sure that you are as great as He is, and that no one could be greater than you." And do you know, some of the angels did—they joined themselves to the first bad angel, whom we call Satan, and they all said, " We will *not* do anything God tells us ! We are just as good and great as He is."

Well, at that the good angels turned on them and there was a great battle in heaven, and the good angels drove the bad ones out and they fell into a place I had made for them —because they had to have somewhere to go ;

a place called Hell. That was the first thing that happened to the first people who wouldn't do what they were told!

Not doing what you are told is called " disobedience ", and it is the first sin there ever was. And just as it was the angels' first sin, so it was the first sin on this earth.

I told you how I made a lovely garden and put Adam and Eve to live there, and that they would have gone on happily living there until it was time to come to heaven, and that they need never have been unhappy, nor even have died on their way to heaven, if only they would have done what they were told. But Satan slipped into the garden disguised as a snake, and told Eve to do just what I had told her *not* to do. There was just one tree in all that

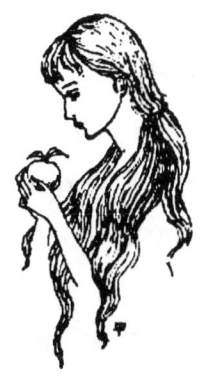

Eve

garden from which they were not to eat the fruit; that was all I asked of them—just to leave that tree alone. But the Devil said to Eve that she would be as grand as God if they ate it, and she believed him. So she ate some, and gave some to Adam, and he ate it—they were disobedient! So they had to leave that lovely garden and go out into the hard, cold world outside. All the trouble in the world from aches and pains to prisons and wars all came into the world because of Adam and Eve being disobedient!

Have you heard it said about me that I was " obedient unto death "? That means I was obedient even when it meant dying. That special obedience of mine was to make up for all the disobedience that began with the Devil and Adam and Eve and has been going on ever since.

You: Being obedient seems to be very important—but shall I have to go on being obedient even when I am grown-up?

Jesus: You will have to go on and on until you die if you want to get to heaven. You will always have to obey me and my Church, and there will always be laws and other people that have to be obeyed, too. The thing to do is to get very good at obeying while you are small. If you get into the way of it now, it will be much easier later on. But if you get into the way of being disobedient now, then it will get harder and harder as you get older, and it may end in your not being friends with me any more.

You: Then I suppose I shall just have to keep on trying, but you must be sure to help me or I shall never manage it at all.

SEVENTH CONVERSATION:

ABOUT HOW DIFFICULT IT IS TO BE OBEDIENT

You: Jesus! Do please come here and help! I have been awful to Mummy, after all you said about doing what you are told. She called me in for dinner when I was in the middle of a game, and I shouted, " I'll come when I'm ready! " and I didn't go in till the game was finished. And then I found dinner was finished, too, and she sent me straight up to my room without any, because she said I couldn't be hungry—and, oh, I am! And besides that, I am so cross and miserable.

Jesus: You see, it is never really worth refusing to obey; it only means being unhappy and making your mummy unhappy, too. Besides, I told you you must practise obeying now, so that it will be easy when you grow up.

You: But, Jesus, it is going on *all day long*— " Pick up your toys ", " Finish your pudding ", " Come in at once ", " Change your shoes ", " Sit up properly ", " Time for bed " —my goodness, there's no end to it, and I am always having to stop right in the middle of something specially interesting to do something else!

Jesus: I know—indeed I do! And it is like that all through life—no matter how grown-up and grand you may become, you will never quite have time for all the things you really want to do. There is only one way of not minding too much. Shall I tell you about it?

You: Yes, please—if I could only remember in time!

Jesus: Perhaps you will be able to remember this—some of the time, any way. You are fond of your mother, really, aren't you?

You: Why, of course I am—and of my father, too.

Jesus: Then when one of them asks you to do something for them when you are in the middle of a game, just think quickly, " Do I really love this game better than my mummy ? Or better than my daddy? " which ever it is.

You: Yes, that would help, because of course I don't love the game as much as all that really. But it wouldn't be any help when somebody I don't like tells me to do something I don't want to.

Jesus: What about me? Couldn't you remember that even if you are not at all fond of that person, I am? I love even people you don't like, even people nobody likes very much, more than you love your mummy and daddy.

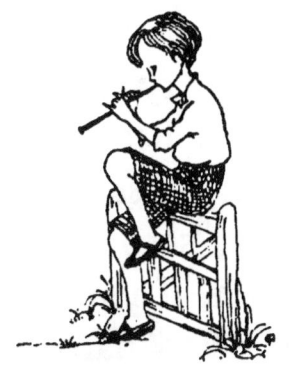

A little noise

You: Oh, Jesus, it's all very well, but you can't really love Miss Smith—you know her, the old lady who lives next door and makes such a fuss about a little noise—you can't really love her more than I love Mummy? I don't see how you can!

Jesus: Although I am so small, my heart is very, very large. There is room in it for everybody in the world. If you want to be friends with me you must make your own heart larger, so that there is room in yours for everybody, too. You might begin with making a little room for Miss Smith. *You* know when she calls out to you to be quiet for goodness sake and sounds so cross, but only *I* know how often she wants to do that and doesn't, because she is a friend of mine and knows that I am fond of you. She really tries very hard to be nice to you. Do you think, for my sake, you could try and be nice to her?

You: The more I hear about being friends with you, Jesus, the less easy it seems, but I really do want to, so I will try even to be nice to Miss Smith, if you really want me to.

Jesus: It does seem hard to do the things I want; but when you've done them you feel happier. If you will really try to be nice to everybody, because I love them all, then we shall always be friends and I shall never have to send you away from me as I had to send Satan and Adam and Eve.

EIGHTH CONVERSATION:
ABOUT JESUS BEING OBEDIENT

Jesus: We are specially good friends today! Here you are in bed, and I know you have been doing what you were told all day long. Even when you were told you could not have any more ice-cream you didn't make a fuss!

You: You know, Jesus, Mummy looked so surprised and pleased, it was worth it, and I knew you were watching and being pleased, too.

Jesus: So I was. And if you could see what I gave you instead of the ice-cream you would be more pleased still!

You: Oh, Jesus, what was it?

Jesus: Ah! I am not going to tell you! But it was something I added to the storehouse of treasure that is waiting for you in heaven.

28

When you see it you will say, " But this is worth all the ice-cream in the world, and I only gave up one helping! " And I shall remind you, " Yes, obedience when it is difficult is worth all that! "

You: Jesus, do you really mean that there is a whole heap of lovely things waiting for me in heaven, and that you add something to it every time I am good ?

Jesus: That is just what I mean. Only be sure you stay friends with me and come to heaven, or I shall have to give it all to somebody else, and I do not want that to happen at all. There is plenty of treasure for everybody in heaven, if only everybody would take the trouble to come and get it.

You: Well, I shall certainly get there if I can. Jesus, you know I have been good today, but you know how nearly I wasn't once or twice. Tell me some more about how you managed to be good, or perhaps tomorrow I shall be worse than ever after working so hard to be good today.

Jesus: The Gospels are four books my friends wrote about me. One of them tells about my being obedient, all in five words: " He was

29

subject to them." That means I always did what my mother and St. Joseph told me to. There was plenty for me to do when I was Our Lady's little boy at Nazareth, and plenty of other things I would rather have done. My

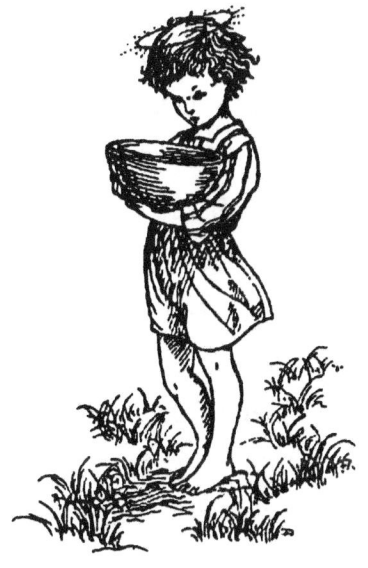

Jesus fetching water

mother would call, " Jesus! Just run and fetch some water from the well! " And I went at once and came back as fast as I could without spilling it and said, " Do you want anything else, Mummy? " when I got there. That sounds very easy, but often I would rather have gone on playing with our kitten or hearing a story St. Joseph was telling me,

30

or making a boat from the chips of wood in his shop.

Or St. Joseph would tell me, " Don't touch those nails—they are a special sort and I have only just enough for the cupboard I am making." And then he would go away and I would want very much to have one of those long straight nails for the mast of my boat, but I didn't take one. It was easier for me than for you in one way, because I was God and the Devil had no hold on me. But it was harder in another way, because I could so easily have made more nails just like the ones I was not to touch. I could have made them, just as I made the world, out of nothing, just by telling them to be there. But I never did that. I practised being obedient instead. When you want to disobey, you might remember that, too. I was God and I practised being obedient just as you have to, because I had come into the world to be obedient and to die in obedience to my Father.

That's why the cross I died on is the very best thing to look at or think about when you don't want to do what you are told. There is a cross in your room and one on the Church and one on your mummy's rosary, and if you can't see any of those when you are tempted to be bad, shut your eyes and think of it. That is a plan that works very well for everybody—children and grown-ups, too.

You: Well, I will remember that. But Jesus, did that really happen to you—having to go and do things for people when you were busy with a game? And did you have to come indoors suddenly because there were visitors? The very worst thing about visitors is that they always come just when you specially wish they wouldn't!

Jesus: Of course that happened to me—it happens to everybody! And it doesn't stop happening when you grow up. Your mother often wishes people wouldn't come in to see her just when she is in the middle of making a cake or ironing your clothes, but it will happen. You see how nice she always is to them, just like my mother was, and if you are to be friends with me you must manage to be nice, too.

You: Well, I'll try, but I hope they won't do it too often.

Jesus: So did I, and so does everyone! But however difficult it is always to try to be nice to everyone, you know very well that you are much happier when you manage it than when you don't. It is really a help if you remember that I love all these tiresome people much more than anyone else does, so when you are nice to them I am specially pleased. If someone said they were friends with you and then were horrid to your mother, you wouldn't want to be friends with them very much, would you?

You: I should think not!

Jesus: Why?

You: Well, because I am very, very fond of my mummy, and I wouldn't want to be friends with anyone who wasn't nice to her.

Jesus: There, you see! I am very, very fond of everybody in the world, so if you want to be friends with me you must be nice to everybody.

You: How can you be fond of everybody? Even the bad ones?

Jesus: Well, you see, when I grew up I died for them, even the horrid ones, so that they could have a chance of heaven, and I wouldn't have bothered, would I, if I hadn't been fond of them?

You: Well then, Jesus, I have to put up with visitors who interrupt and are a nuisance, and I have to be nice to Mummy and Daddy. That part of it isn't hard, anyway.

Jesus: Isn't it? I wonder if you do it as well as ever you can? When your daddy comes home in the evening do you run to meet him and ask him if he wants you to bring him anything?

You: Well, no. You see, I am generally out playing when he comes home. But if he calls me for anything, I go.

Jesus: Don't you think he would rather like it if you sometimes went without being asked?

You: Yes, I expect he would.

Jesus: You try it and see. I used to go to our carpenter's shop to tell my daddy when supper was ready, and he liked me to come and wait while he put his tools away and then walk back to our house with him. And after supper I helped my mummy clear away and do the dishes. Do you do that?

You: I don't much like doing dishes.

Jesus: Neither did I! But I loved my mother and didn't see why she should have to do them all by herself—she didn't like doing dishes either!—and, after all, she had been working hard all day. And afterwards, before I went to bed, I used to sit beside her while she did the mending and she used to tell me stories or sing songs for me. My father used to listen, too, and sometimes he told me stories about when he was a little boy. You know, we were the happiest three people in all the world. And it wasn't just because I was God—it was because we were always as nice as ever we could be to each other and to everyone else.

NINTH CONVERSATION:

WHAT JESUS DID ABOUT OBEDIENCE

You: Jesus, it mayn't be so easy to be friends with you as I thought at first, but you are so nice I can't imagine anybody being really horrid to you. How could anyone have been so beastly to you—fancy nailing you to a cross and letting you die there! I wouldn't do that to anyone at all, even if I didn't like them, and I don't believe anyone I know would either. Anyhow, why did you *let* them?

Jesus: It is difficult to explain about it, but

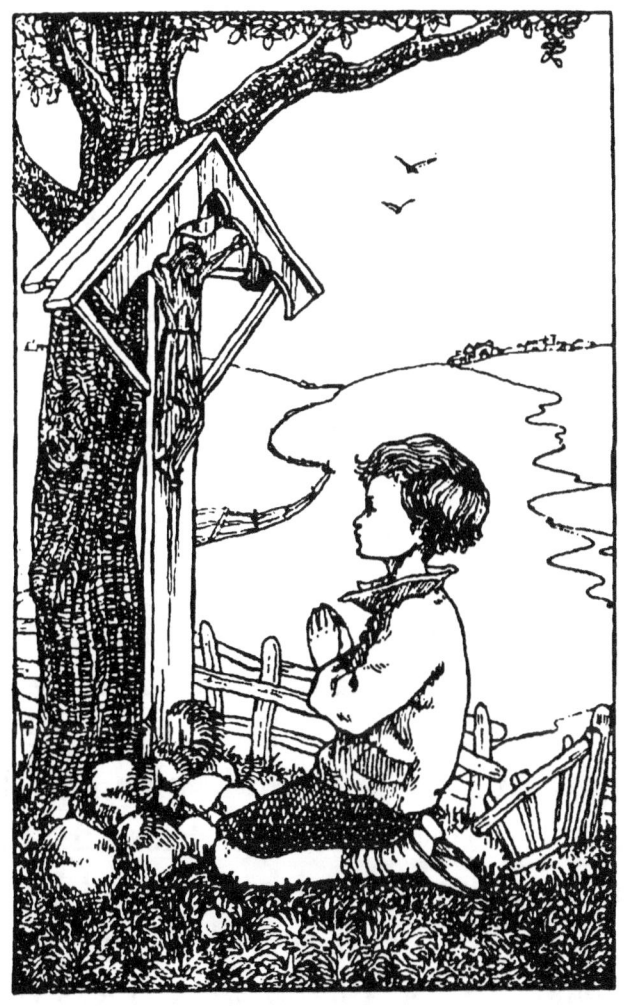

The Crucifix

I will try to, if you will try to understand, because you won't really know me well until you do understand. And I very much want you to understand as well as ever you can. I told you how badly Adam and Eve behaved in Paradise, how they wouldn't obey me, and how wicked some of the angels were even before that. Between them they had shut the doors of heaven on everyone in the world. But they hadn't shut them out of my love. I still loved everyone in the world and wanted them all to come to heaven, but there was nothing they could do to get there, unless I helped them. So the Blessed Trinity (that's my Father, the Holy Ghost and me), who you know are all one God, planned that I, the second Person of the Blessed Trinity, should come down from heaven and be a man as well as God. You see, if I were a man I could make up for all the wickedness of men, and because I would go on being God, too, my making up would be really worth as much as it need be to get Adam's sin forgiven, and all the other sins that had happened since then. So that was what I did : I came and was first a baby, then a boy, then a man, and at last died, all to make up by my obedience for all the disobediences in the world.

So I was born, as you know, as Our Lady's baby, and grew up at Nazareth, and when I had grown up I went about teaching people all the things about me that had been forgotten since Adam first learnt them, and making up by my obedience for all their disobedience.

You: But they ought to have been so pleased! That doesn't explain at all why they should want to kill you!

Jesus: They had forgotten too much, and been disobedient too often. Oftener than you can imagine.

You: When I am disobedient I am punished.

Jesus: So is everyone else. My Father tried to cure the world of being disobedient again and again, by punishing them. Once he sent a flood of water upon the earth, and drowned mankind except the one good man who was left, and his family. You know the story about Noah? How God warned him what was going to happen, and told him how to make a great ship, like a house, with room in it for him and his wife and his sons and their wives and pairs of all kinds of animals.

When it began to rain Noah and his family and the animals all went into the boat (it was called Noah's Ark) and it floated on the water, and they were saved. The flood lasted for weeks, and when they came out again and found they were the only people left in the world, and knew why, you would have thought they would be sure to obey God and teach their children, too, wouldn't you? But it didn't work out like that. Soon everybody forgot all about what can happen if you don't obey God, and they began to be wicked again. They stopped worshipping God and worshipped silly pretending gods they made out of wood and stone and things instead. By the time I came they were just as bad as ever. Too many of the people who made the laws and saw that they were kept thought this world much more important than the next, and that what the man said who was the very greatest king in the world, was more important than what God said.

You: Who was the greatest king in the world?

Jesus: Cæsar, he was called. He lived in Rome, and he had conquered the country

where I came to live, as well as a great many
other countries. There was a Roman called
Pontius Pilate who was governor of my country,
and my people thought that I should fight him
and conquer him, and make our country our
own again, and reign there for ever as a great
king. When they found that I didn't mean to
do that at all, they didn't want to have anything more to do with me. And yet they were
frightened of me, too, because heaps and heaps
of ordinary people who didn't make laws, and
a few even of those who did, followed me and
were ready to do anything I told them. They
believed in me, and it is always the way that
those who do not believe in me do not want
anyone else to believe in me either, and are
suspicious of those who do. Besides, they
had heard that I claimed to be God, and that
was too much for them altogether.

You: I don't see why, when you did things
like bringing dead people to life again.

Jesus: They didn't want to believe it, and
no one will ever believe what they don't want
to. You see, if it were really true that I was
God, they knew they would have to do as I
told them, and admit that I was greater than

they were. They simply couldn't bear the idea of that! So they went to Pontius Pilate and told him I was plotting against Cæsar and ought to be put to death. Pontius Pilate didn't believe them, so then they came out with the real truth, that I had claimed to be God, and ought to be killed for that. At first Pontius Pilate was frightened when he heard that, in case it were true. But then the rulers of my people went back to the first charge and said, " Anyhow, he is plotting against Cæsar, and if you don't have him put to death we shall tell Cæsar about it and you will lose your job." So Pontius Pilate decided that nothing worse than that could happen to him, and that Cæsar was really more important than God, anyway, but he still didn't want to have me killed. So he made his soldiers beat me instead. They beat me till my back was all bleeding and I could hardly stand up, and then Pilate brought me out on a balcony of his house to show to them. He thought that if they saw how awful I looked they would be sorry for me and willing for Pilate to let me go. But they weren't a bit sorry for me; they shouted out,

" Crucify him! Crucify him! " Pilate was more frightened of what they would tell Cæsar than he was of God, so he gave orders that I should be crucified.

You: How could he be so horrid?

Jesus: He didn't think it mattered very much if I were not God, and if I were he didn't think I would let myself be crucified.

You: Well, why did you? You could have made all your enemies fall down dead, and then everyone would have known you were God, and surely then they would have been good.

Jesus: But before I ever came down from heaven to be Our Lady's baby I knew just how it would be, and I had planned that what I would do to make up for the disobedience of the world would be to die obediently on a cross. It would have spoilt everything if I had refused to do it at the last minute.

You: But why did you plan anything so awful? Wouldn't something less have done?

Jesus: Of course it would. But I chose to do it that way, for just one reason.

You: What was that?

42

Jesus: Just so people could *never* say, " God doesn't really love us," or, " It's easy enough for *Him* to love us," or, " What does *He* know about trouble and pain and sorrow ? " or, " I don't think God really minds about sin." You can't possibly say any of those things, can you? Because I died such an awful death just to show that I do love you, and do hate sin, and do want you all in heaven as badly as all *that.* And I'll tell you something else, as you are a friend of mine.

You: What else, Jesus?

Jesus: If there had been only one person in all the world, I would have died for him just the same.

You: My goodness, Jesus, do you really mean that you would have done all that for just one person—anyone at all?

Jesus: Anyone at all. If there had been no one in the world except you I would have done it just the same.

PART III

TENTH CONVERSATION:
ABOUT BEING HAPPY

Jesus: Here is the sun shining and the wind blowing, and you are out in the garden among all kinds of flowers that I made to please you, and you look sad!

You: Of course I am sad. I keep remembering all the awful things that happened to you

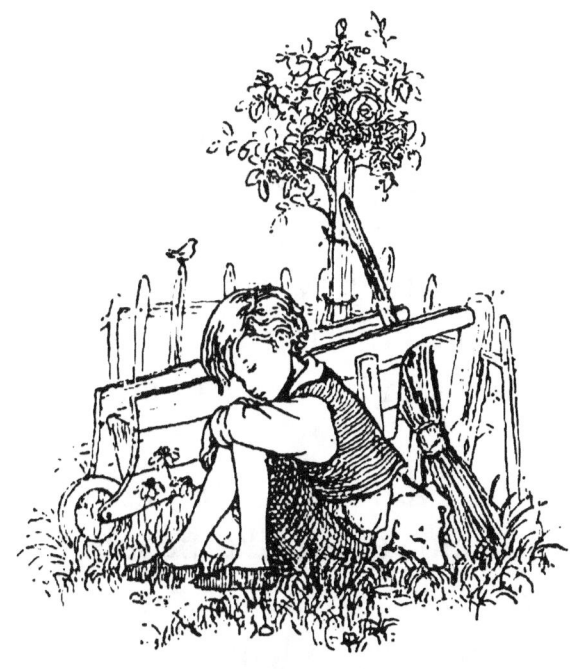

Looking sad

after you grew up. How can anyone think of you being killed like that and not be sad?

Jesus: I can, and so can you. Remembering my cross is not meant to make you miserable. You know very well that after I had been lying dead in the tomb from Good Friday evening to Sunday morning I came alive again, and after I had been to see my mother and all my friends I went up to heaven to my Father. So when you remember my sufferings you are to think that through them and some smaller ones of your own you are to come up to heaven, too, and be happy with me for ever. I have told you how much I went through for you, so that you will know what a lot you are worth to me, and so that you will be cheerful and willing when I ask you to go through a little suffering for me—it won't be more than you can be cheerful about, you may be sure.

You: Then I am not to be sad?

Jesus: I do not at all like people to be sad. All my very best friends have always been extra happy and cheerful, and so should you be.

There is a sham sort of goodness that means going about with a long face and talking about

45

how many prayers you say—a sort of imitation goodness that makes you think of a wet day.

I don't like that sort at all. I like the real sort of goodness that is extra happy and makes you think of sunshine and laughter. Remember, I always knew all my life what was going to happen to me, and I was not sad. I knew I had a Father in heaven looking after me, besides a very loving mother and father on earth. We were very happy at Nazareth, and so should you be.

If you are much with me you will soon learn that being good goes with being happy. And if you think before you do anything you are not sure you ought to do, " Would my friend Jesus like me to do this, or not? " then you will be sure to choose right.

You: Our teacher in school says Johnny is good, and I can't bear him!

Jesus: He is not good now, though he manages to make some grown-ups think he is. I wish he would *really* make friends with me, instead of only pretending to. As it is, he wears a long face, tells tales about the other children, and is always planning to

46

show everybody how good and clever he is. I don't like that sort of thing at all, and I promise you it has nothing to do with being good.

You: You make it sound much easier to be good than I find it when I try. But I'm glad I don't have to be like Johnny.

Jesus: Being good gets easier as you go on, like anything else. If you try to do something like learning to read, it seems very difficult at first; but after a time, if you keep trying, it begins to get easier. And remember, that heap of treasure I have for you in heaven will be growing all the time. But even now you often have a reward. When your mother smiles at you in the evening and says, "You have been as good as gold today!" isn't that a lovely feeling?

When I was playing at Nazareth and looked up and saw my mother watching me, I would think, " There is Mummy smiling and I know she is saying to herself, ' My Jesus is so happy and so good.' "

ELEVENTH CONVERSATION:
ABOUT NOT GETTING CROSS

You: Jesus! I have been so cross! I was quite all right, sailing a boat on the water butt in the garden, and then the mast came out and went down to the bottom and I couldn't reach it, and then I stepped on my boat when I was trying to, so then I got cross and threw the old boat away as hard as I could and Mummy was just coming round the corner and it hit her in the face and she said, " Good gracious! What *is* the matter! " and I was too cross to explain and stamped my foot and ran into the house, and now I am sorry I can't tell her so, because she has gone shopping. Isn't it all miserable?

Jesus: Never mind, you have told me you are sorry, and you will tell your mummy the same as soon as ever you can, so cheer up. But I must tell you that really good friends of mine manage not to get into such silly tempers. It is silly, and ugly, and it only makes everybody unhappy. It often ends in something being broken, or somebody being hurt. I

48

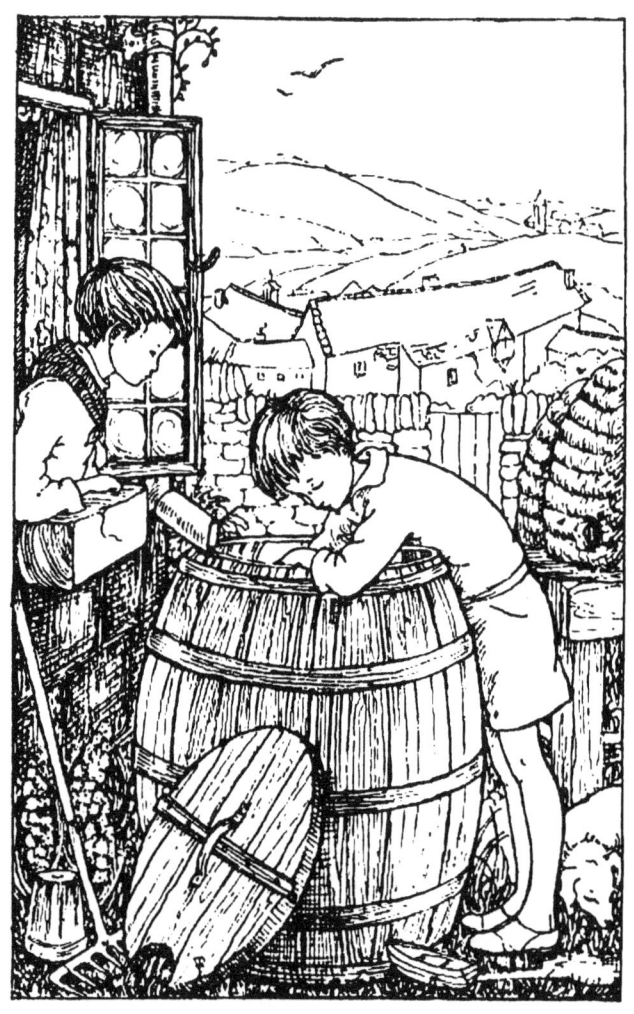

Sailing a boat on the water butt

have known boys who kick their own dog, just because they are cross. Sometimes the dog bites them, and quite right, too. And there are some children who throw toy soldiers across the room when they won't stand up—as if they were more likely to stand up after that!

I have known little girls who bang on the piano with their fists when they make a mistake, playing scales, and some others who make a terrific scene when their hair is combed. And I am afraid boys are no better. My Father and I from heaven have heard this fuss going on every morning since the world began, and it does not please us at all. Do you think I gave you a voice so that you could howl and scream when things do not go exactly as you would like them to? You know very well I gave it to you so that you could talk sensibly and sing. You can sing for me whenever you like; I like to hear you sing.

And then your hands and feet. Do you suppose I gave you those so that you could knock things about and kick when you are angry? Of course I didn't! I gave you hands so that you could work and play with them, and I gave you feet so that you could stand up on them and run and dance and jump. When your life is finished and you come to the gate of heaven, my Father and I will ask you how you have used the hands and feet we gave you. If you have to say, " For hitting and kicking and tearing and stamping, mostly," you need not suppose that we shall be pleased.

Do you know what beautiful things eyes are? Well, I did not give you yours so that you could glare like an angry bull, but so that you could see all the lovely things I made for you to look at.

I did not give you a nose to wrinkle up and make faces with, I gave it to you so that you could breathe the fresh air and smell my lovely flowers.

And your mouth, which opens and shuts so cleverly, is meant for talking and smiling and eating—not for screaming and grinding your teeth!

You: Jesus, I'm good now; do stop about all those silly things—I know very well that being cross is silly, and I will try not to any more.

Jesus: Please do—not only because you want to be friends with me, but also because you do not like to be laughed at, and when children are cross, or grown-ups for that matter, everybody else wants to laugh. It is only the cross person who doesn't see how funny they look with their lower lip stuck out and their backs turned to everybody, and their faces screwed up to look as ugly as they possibly can. Some children will go on behaving like that for hours at a time, but I know one person who has been sulking for the longest of all.

You: Who is that?

Jesus: Why, the Devil, of course! He has been sulking ever since he was turned out of heaven, and he is the only person who is pleased to see a child sulking. " Ah," he says then, " there is a child who is beginning to look like me already—how delightful! " And children who the Devil is pleased with are taking a first step towards being very like him indeed.

TWELFTH CONVERSATION:
ABOUT SWEETS AND THINGS

You: Jesus, do you like sweets?

Jesus: Yes, very much, specially the ones my mother used to make for feast days—they were simply lovely, much better than the ones I could buy in the sweet shop, though those were very good, too.

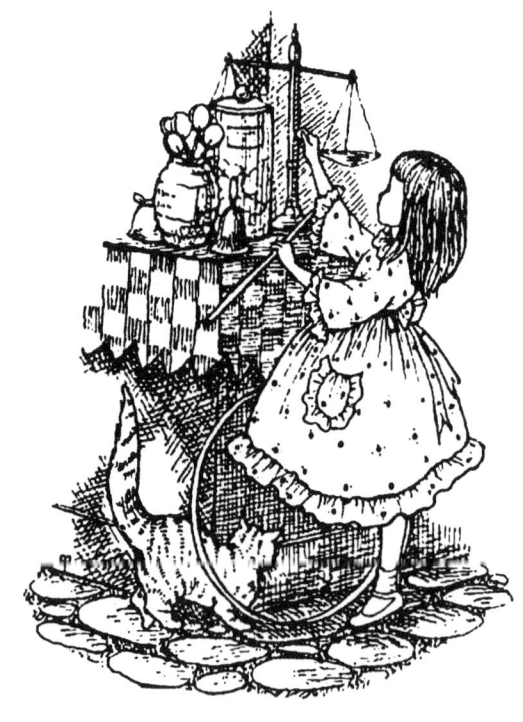

Sweets

53

You: And did you like oranges and melons and strawberries?

Jesus: There was lovely fruit in Nazareth and I loved it just as much as you do. Why do you suppose I made fruit so good if it was not so that everyone should enjoy it?

You: Did you really make it for us to enjoy? And nuts, and cream and honey, and all the other things that are so wonderfully good to eat?

Jesus: I made them all for you to enjoy, and enjoyed them very much myself when I came into the world. And, just like you, I had to remember that too much of any of them would mean bad dreams and being sick.

You: That's just the trouble, Jesus. I know that, too, but it is very difficult to remember in time when you are enjoying them.

Jesus: But your mummy tells you when to stop, just as mine told me!

You: But when she isn't there . . .

Jesus: Then you know how much she would say you might have, don't you?

You: Yes, I do really. But it's much easier to think, " Just one more won't matter," than to stop when you ought.

Jesus: I'll tell you what to do then. Just think quickly, " Which do I *really* love most: my mummy, or these good things to eat? " And remember that I am beside you hoping so much that you will remember to stay friends with me—being greedy is not at all the way I like my friends to behave! And you feel so silly, too, if you do eat too much of them and feel sick afterwards, and have to have medicine, and it's all your own fault!

You: Well, I will try to do that, but it's very difficult.

Jesus: I know it is; it's just one of those things you have to keep on trying about. But, anyhow, don't ever be one of those children who steal sweets and then tell lies about it when they don't want to eat their dinner afterwards.

And don't be like those other children who nearly pull their mother's arm off when she is going past the sweet shop. You can't expect to stay friends with me if you behave like that.

You: I don't mind so much, anyway, if you really know how nice those things are and meant us to enjoy them.

Jesus: I did indeed—I made the whole world and everything in it for you to be happy in, and so you will if you use the things I made as I meant you to. I made sleep, too, to divide one day from the next, so that the new one is lovely and fresh, and you are all new and rested to enjoy it. I don't like it at all when people don't want to get up in the morning, though. There are not many children like that—most of them want to get up as soon as they are awake. But going to bed is another matter.

You: Oh, getting up is easy, except that washing and dressing are a nuisance; but it is always time to go to bed before I am ready.

Jesus: I know, specially in summer—it used to be so lovely at home in the evenings, I wanted to stay out and play all night! And if I couldn't do that (and of course I couldn't), then, anyhow, I wanted to play till the very last moment and leave all the things I had been playing with on the ground just where they were. But I didn't, and you need not, you know—it is all part of being obedient, which I was always practising and which you must be practising, too. It is better in the end to pick your things up and put them away, anyhow. You aren't pleased in the morning, are you, to find the things you should have put away the night before have been trodden on or swept up, or, if you left them out of doors, that it has rained in the night and spoilt them?

You: Like the aeroplane I was given for my birthday—I left it out one night and in the morning I found our dog had chewed it all out of shape.

Jesus: So you were cross with the dog— but it was all your own fault! Putting things away is a great nuisance, but it's one of the things you have to learn to do when you are young, otherwise you won't do it when you are grown-up and then you will be a special sort of nuisance to everybody all your life. What do you think would happen, anyway, if grown-ups usually did leave the things they have been using just where they were when they had finished with them? What about a real aeroplane if that were just left on the field where it came down, and not put away and attended to? What if horses were left in their carts all night? Or if your mummy were to leave everything just where it was in the kitchen when she had finished cooking and never clear everything away? Clearing the table and doing the dishes after dinner is a tiresome thing, but what would it be like if they were all left dirty on the table from one meal to the next?

You see, being told to put things away is another thing that seems as if it had been invented just to annoy children, but really if the world is to run smoothly it is something everybody has to do all the time. Even after people die someone else has to put their bodies neatly away to wait till the end of the world! But if you stay friends with me, then I promise you that when your body is put away for you you shall come up to heaven with me, and in heaven no one ever has to put anything away!

THIRTEENTH CONVERSATION:
ABOUT LESSONS

You: There is one thing, anyway, Jesus, that children have to put up with that doesn't bother grown-ups. Lessons! I have begun to go to school, and it's awful—we have to learn things and do things all day long, and even when we come home we have to learn another lesson for next day!

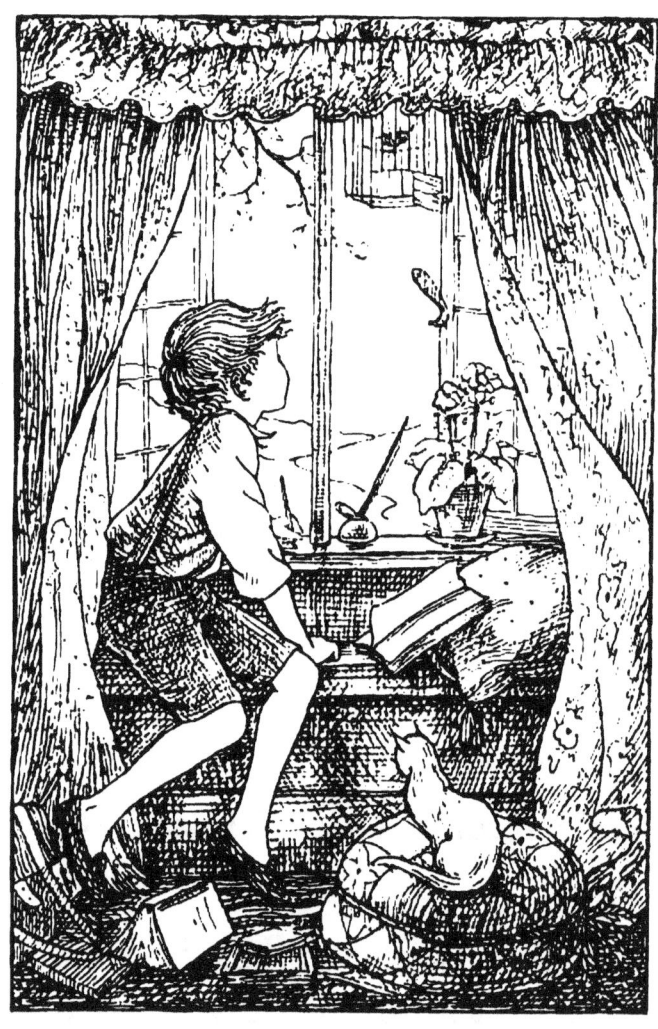

Homework

Jesus: Lessons are just the kind of work children do, and nearly all grown-ups have to work, and most of them find the work they do just as difficult and tiresome as you find lessons. Your father goes out to work all day, and he often wishes and wishes he need not; and your mother has to work just as hard keeping the house clean and doing the shopping and cooking and looking after your clothes. And do you know who invented all this trouble?

You: If I did know, I would get even with him!

Jesus: I hope you will—it was the Devil! But he could not have done it without the help of Adam and Eve. Hard work was part of the punishment God gave Adam and Eve after they disobeyed him in the lovely garden he had made for them. The Devil suggested that disobedience, you remember—he told them they would be just as clever as God if they disobeyed him and ate the fruit from the tree they had been told to leave alone.

You: And if they hadn't, I should not have had to do lessons?

Jesus: You would have learned things, but there would have been no trouble about it;

60

it would have been easy and fun all the time. Adam had to work in the garden, you know, before the Devil appeared, but it was easy and he enjoyed it, and never had to work till he was really tired. Now nearly everybody has to work harder than they want to, and learning things, instead of being as much fun as a game, is very hard work indeed.

You: I do wish I had been Adam—I should never have been so silly!

Jesus: Are you sure you would not? Haven't you ever done anything when you knew you ought not to—even when you knew you would be sorry afterwards?

You: Well, yes, I have, of course. Lots of times.

Jesus: Then don't be too sure you wouldn't have failed just as Adam did. After all, he was sorry afterwards, and came up to heaven with me at last. But be as angry as you like with the Devil! And show him that you mean to obey God by accepting His punishment and doing your lessons as well as ever you can.

And you can remember that I did lessons, too, even very dull ones, when I would much rather not have. Just to show you it is worth being obedient, I learnt all I was told to—it was rather a joke really, when I was sat down to learn a piece out of the Bible. I had known all about it before it was written, you know, and it was I who saw to it that it *was* written. But I learned it all just the same. And I did sums, too, and learned all sorts of things that I didn't at all want to learn or need to know. So just remember, when you have to do lessons that seem very difficult and tiresome, and all about something very uninteresting, " Jesus did lessons, too, and he will help me get this right." And so I will.

You: Jesus, it is funny to think of you doing lessons!

Jesus: Yes, isn't it? I had made everything, you know—even the people who were teaching me—besides all the things I was learning about. I did it, as I told you, just to show that doing what you are told is always worth while.

But you do really need to know the things you learn in school if you are to be a really useful man when you grow up, and the harder you try the better friends we shall be. Remember, you don't need to win all the prizes to please me, only to try hard. Even if you keep finding yourself at the bottom of the class, I won't mind a bit so long as you were really trying.

You: Very well, I'll try, and you will help me, and if I am very stupid I will say, " Well, I did try, anyway, so Jesus is pleased," and when I am clever I will say, " Thank you, Jesus, for helping me."

FOURTEENTH CONVERSATION:

ABOUT WHAT YOUR SOUL IS LIKE

Jesus: Do you know what a soul is like?

You: No. I know I have one, but I don't know what it looks like because I can't see it. What is it like?

Jesus: No one else can see it either; it is one of the things I made that no eye can see, but only God. But if your soul were something you could see it might be like a big white flower. There are stories you know of fairies living in flowers, but they are only stories. But your soul is like a flower with a little room in the centre of it—a little room

63

where somebody really does live. Do you know who?

You: No, I didn't know anybody did.

Jesus: I do! When you were baptised I drove the Devil away from your clean new white soul, made specially for you, and I came to live there. That's really why it is so easy for you to talk to me, even though you can't see me—there I am, right in your own soul!

Now, we have been talking about all the things that can drive me away—things like disobedience, and greediness, laziness and self-ishness and bad temper. Sometimes those things just spoil my home in your soul, like a slug spoils a lily, but if you go on being as bad as you know how till you are really wicked, then I shall be driven out and the Devil will come to visit you instead. I hope you would not like that.

You: Jesus, how awful! please don't ever let that happen! But can he come without my wanting him to?

Jesus: He can only come if you first drive me away and will not let me come back. So long as we are friends he can never hurt you at all, you may be quite sure of that; and if you should ever be really wicked and drive me away, and the Devil should come instead, then you have only really to want me back, only to be really sorry you sent me away, and I will come back again. You need not be afraid— I am much stronger than the Devil, and so is my mother and your guardian angel!

But do not let nasty little sins like slugs spoil my home in your soul, thinking, " This will be a sin, but only a little one—perhaps hardly a sin at all, really," or, " This isn't true, but it's only a little lie," or, " Just this time I am not going to try to be good."

You: But, Jesus, there are so many different kinds of sins, and sometimes things turn out to be sins that I did not really think were wrong—how am I to be sure?

Jesus: If you remember that I am with you in your soul's little room, you need only turn round to me in your mind and say, " Is this something I would do if I could see Jesus standing beside me? " You will not make many mistakes; but if you are still not sure, than ask your mummy or ask the priest when you go to confession. If you say, " I have done something that might be wrong, but I am not sure," he and I will soon set you right about it, and then you will know next time.

You: And if I do that, will you promise not to go away?

Jesus: I never go away from anyone who really wants me to stay, and so long as I am there I am not idle.

You: What do you do, in my soul?

Jesus: When you do not keep me too busy cleaning up the traces of sins, I work at making it a more and more lovely soul, more shining, with new colours—more like the soul you must have if you are to come and live in heaven at last.

But there is somewhere else I live besides in your soul, and in a different way. Do you know where that is?

You: In church?

Jesus: Yes, in a cup made of silver or gold, in the little house in the middle of the altar in church.

You: Your little house in church is called the tabernacle, isn't it?

Jesus: Yes, and the cup is called the ciborium.

66

There I am for you to come and talk to whenever you like. But don't forget that though I am in my little house in church in a very special way that I am going to tell you more about some time, I am really and truly in your soul, too. And just as my room on the altar, and everything about it, has to be kept as clean as clean and as neat and lovely as possible, so you ought to keep your soul always fresh and clean and fit for me to live in. If you remember that, it will be much easier to be good.

Prayer

Please, Jesus, stay in my soul always and make it a place where you like to be. And help me not to spoil it.

My guardian angel, please keep guard over my soul and don't let anything interfere with Jesus in it.

St. Joseph, you looked after Jesus and took care of him when he was your little boy at Nazareth. Please go on taking care of him in my soul.

Our Lady, please help St. Joseph, and keep Jesus safe, and don't let me ever do anything that will drive him away. When the Devil comes creeping round to play tricks on me, send him away quick, and help me to show him that I do not want to have anything to do with him at all, ever.

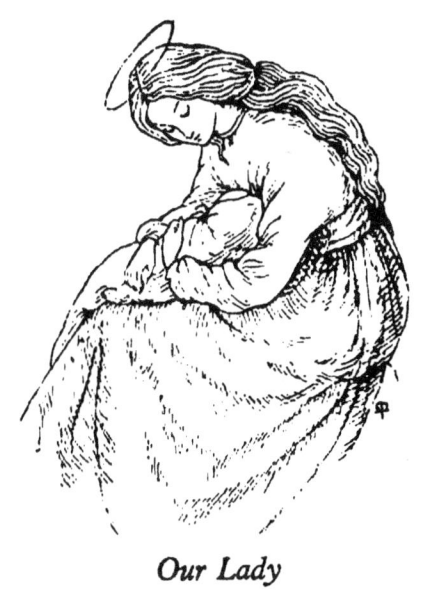

Our Lady

FIFTEENTH CONVERSATION:

ABOUT REMEMBERING TO SAY THANK YOU TO JESUS

Jesus: I really think this is one of the loveliest days I ever made. My birds are singing at the tops of their voices, and the first wild roses (aren't you glad I thought of making roses?) are just coming out! What do you say?

You: It *is* a lovely day.

Jesus: Is that all? Aren't you going to say thank you?

You: Oh yes! Thank you very much for making such a lovely world and such a lovely day!

Jesus: Do you know, so few people say thank you to me for lovely days. Or for the care I took to make wheat for them to make bread with, and sugar cane and fruit so they could have jam on it! Everything you have to eat and wear and play with is made from the lovely things that grow on the earth, like plants, or from animals that run about, or it is dug out of the earth itself where I have stored it for you. And people so seldom stop to say thank you.

When things go wrong and it is colder than they like, or too hot, or things do not grow well, they never forget to complain and blame me, but that isn't my fault.

You: Whose fault is it?

Jesus: It goes back to poor old Adam again— no one would have had anything in the world to complain of if he had not been disobedient. But even now, people have a great deal more to be grateful for than they ever remember. But you will remember, won't you, to say thank you when you see something very nice that I made?

You: Yes, I will. I'll remember you made the sea and the flowers and birds and everything.

Jesus: You have a new kitten in your house, haven't you?

You: Jesus, he is the nicest kitten—he is white with black spots and a black tail and one black ear, and he has a little black mark on his face that is just like a little moustache.

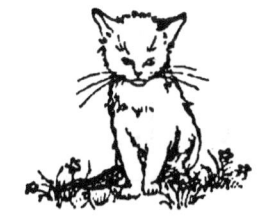

The kitten with the black tail

Jesus: You know, when I planned that kitten I laughed just as you are doing and thought how you would like a kitten with a moustache!

You: Thank you, Jesus, for making me such a funny kitten.

Jesus: He was fun for me, too. But do you think you could always remember that I planned this wonderful world for you and everybody to enjoy, and that it is ungrateful to forget that? So many people forget. Then they treat my world as if I had nothing to do with it, and instead of letting it show them how carefully I planned everything for them, and instead of loving everything in it, because I made it, they forget all about me. They let the things in the world hide me from them, and never think of anything but how they can use my world to make them rich and to amuse them. They get so interested in that that they forget all about heaven and all about me.

You: That's very silly.

Jesus: You can't think how silly it looks from heaven or how pleased the Devil is when he sees it happening. It comes to this at last, that they are afraid to die, because they are only interested in this world and want to stay here for ever. If they only knew how much lovelier heaven is!

You: Jesus, you don't think I shall turn into one of those people, do you?

Jesus: If you will just remember two things you never will: to thank me for what you like in this world, and to remember that heaven is so much better still that it's worth anything at all to get there! If you remember that, then you won't ever let anything you like here prevent you from coming to heaven.

SIXTEENTH CONVERSATION:
ABOUT JESUS' FRIENDS

You: Jesus, I think it's very odd that more people don't want to do what you like. I don't mean just so as to get to heaven, but because you are so nice and so easy to talk to, besides dying for us and everything. Surely nearly everybody who knows you must like you very much indeed?

Jesus: There are a lot of people in this world who know me and are my friends, and a great many who do not know me very well and do not specially want to be friends with me. And others who do not know anything about me really at all. Which ones are which no one really knows except me. Though when you meet someone who reminds you of me, that is generally a sign that he is one of my friends, because my friends grow like me.

You: How do they get like you?

Jesus: Mostly in ways that don't show at all, but a little in ways that do. All of them are people who manage to be happy even when things go wrong for them, and people who make you feel happy when you are with them. You will meet many of my friends in your lifetime, and you will get to recognise them more easily as you grow more like me, too.

Some of them are mothers and fathers who have to work hard and who you would not think had time to think much of me; some of them are people who never got married but who have to be busy all the same; and some are people who have given up the whole of their lives to doing my work.

You: Have I ever met any of those yet?

Jesus: Why, yes, of course you have. The priests you meet are all people whose whole business in this world is my business: helping you to get to heaven—they have given up all the other things they might have done just for that. Then there are other kinds of priests called monks, who all live together in a great house, belonging, not to them, but to me. They spend their lives in working and especially in praying, heaps and heaps of prayers, to make up for all the people who don't pray at all.

There are women who do the same, called nuns, and there are other kinds of nuns who spend their lives nursing or teaching or looking after children who have lost their mothers and fathers, or after old people who have no

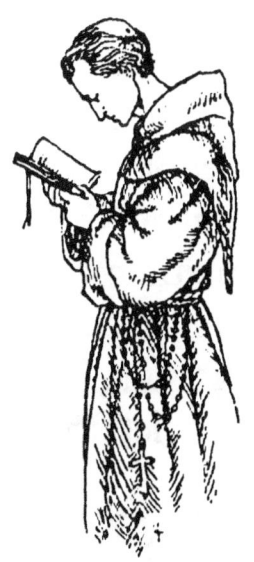

Who spend their lives in prayer

74

children to look after them. You should always be grateful to all these friends of mine and ready to do anything you can for them —but especially you should be grateful to the ones you see least often, the ones whose whole business is prayer. You cannot think what a difference it makes that their prayers are always going up to heaven for all the people who forget to pray!

You: Well, I should think everybody would be grateful to them.

Jesus: But everybody is not—they are very special friends of mine and you will discover as you grow up that special friends of mine have plenty of enemies! When wicked men turn against my Church, those monks and nuns who have been praying for them are always the first people they are angry with. They turn them out of their monasteries and convents, and sometimes kill them, too—the Devil puts that into their heads, of course— you can imagine how he hates such people!

You: But do you let that happen to your friends?

Jesus: Sometimes I do. It only brings them to heaven all the sooner, and with a special crown that is only for people who die for me. There is a whole crowd of them in heaven watching us this moment and smiling because you are so surprised that anyone could have hated them so! I must warn you that if you are my friend you must be willing to die for me if I should ask it of you.

You: And will you take me straight to heaven if I do?

Jesus: In the twinkling of an eye.

You: Then of course I will.

Jesus: Thank you. In the meantime, I am not asking you to do anything as difficult as all that—only to be as good a friend of mine as ever you can. If you do that you shall come to heaven anyway; and on this earth, even though no one knows it, you will come to be a saint. I very much want children to be such friends of mine that they are willing to offer me their lives, to be willing to do anything I ask them.

You: Well, you can have mine to start with. I am not afraid of you asking me to do anything too difficult for me. I know you know just what I can manage, and what I couldn't possibly, even better than I know myself.

So please take my life, and keep it always, and bring me safe to heaven at last.

SEVENTEENTH CONVERSATION:
ABOUT DIAMONDS AND SOULS

Jesus: Thank you for giving me your life. It belongs to me now, and that means it is a holy thing. Something offered to God as you offered me your life is called a Sacrifice. So now your life is a holy sacrifice. When people give me themselves like that, I look at their souls which now belong altogether to me and think how I can make them even more wonderful than they are already. If you will let me, I will make your soul so shining and splendid all the angels will look at it with the greatest delight.

I expect you have seen diamonds. They are little clear stones that sparkle, and so beautiful to look at that people put them in brooches and rings. But to make them sparkle like that they have to be cut and polished so that they catch the light from every direction, as though they were made up of hundreds of tiny mirrors. People look at them and say, " How lovely! " and forget that it took a great deal of work to make them so.

If you let me, I can make your soul like a diamond, catching light from me all over its surface.

You: That would be a lovely kind of soul to have. Is it very difficult for us to begin polishing mine?

Jesus: No, it's not difficult at all. You just have to keep on giving me your life every day, in case you forget whom it belongs to, and to try to be the best friend to me you can: to do all the things I have been telling you about, and not to give up as soon as anything seems difficult. If you do that, your soul will sparkle a little more every day.

You: Could I get a little more sparkle, Jesus, for instance if I helped do the dishes this evening without being asked? And if I stopped asking about whether I shall get what I want for my birthday?

Jesus: Indeed you would. And if you tell your mother very nicely that you are sorry you were cross this morning that would make it shine still more.

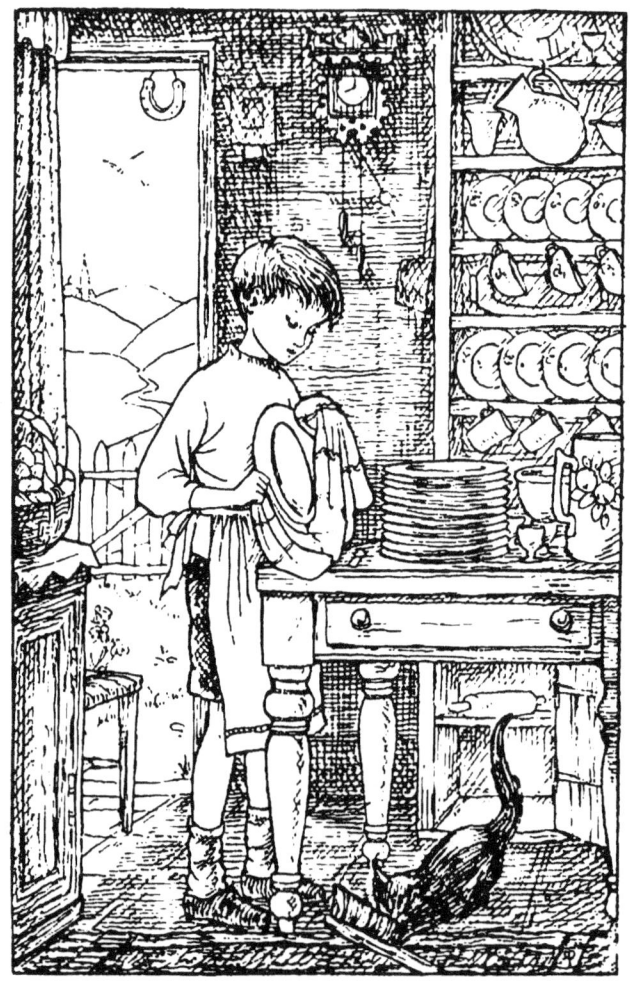

Helping with the dishes

You: Well, none of those things are specially difficult. I might as well begin.

EIGHTEENTH CONVERSATION:
ABOUT THE BLESSED SACRAMENT

You: There now, Jesus, I started off so well, I thought, and then I suddenly got so cross at bedtime! I don't really know now what it was all about, but I was not at all like you.

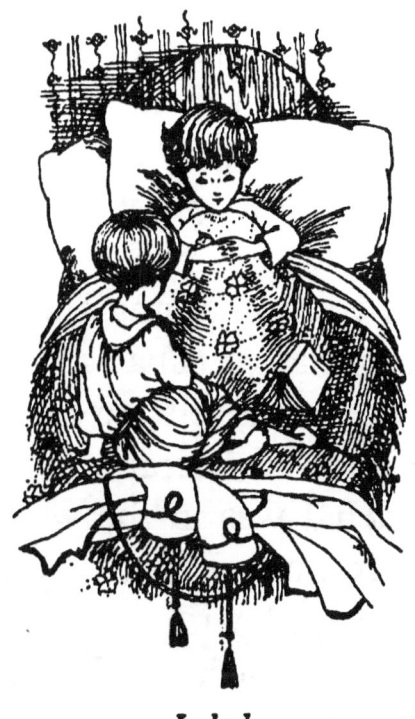

In bed

I was awful! Jesus, what am I to do? I really had been trying and trying to be as good as gold, and then I was as bad as ever after all!

Jesus: Never mind—you were sorry quickly, and you *had* been trying, and now you are all ready to try again. Don't be discouraged when you don't always manage to be good—you will get a little better at it each time you try. And remember, I know all about the times you want to be naughty and manage not to be: nobody else does, *they* only see the times you were naughty in spite of trying!

But I want to tell you more about the gift I have given you to help you to stay friends with me—the greatest gift in all the world.

You: What is it?

Jesus: I told you something about it already. It is my plan so that you shall never be lonely: I gave you my own self, to stay with you always in the Blessed Sacrament.

You see, when I was in the world, and just as big as we are now, I was very fond of the children who played with me. And when I grew up I was still very fond of children, as all nice grown-ups are.

Once when I was going about the country teaching people about how to be friends with God the people with me tried to stop some children from coming up to me because I was so tired. But I said, " No, let them come to me —I made the Kingdom of Heaven for them. Don't ever let them be kept away from me! " When I said that, I thought of you, and of all the other children there would be in the world after I had died and gone back to heaven. I had a plan for them, and I started it working at my last supper on earth. I broke a piece of bread and gave it to my own special friends who were at supper with me, and I said, " This is my body; take it and eat it." And I blessed a cup of wine and told them all to drink it, saying, " This is my blood which is to be shed for you." And I told them to do what I had done, remembering me, till the end of the world.

They knew this was something very mysterious and wonderful and not make-believe, but until after my Father and I sent our Holy Spirit on them at Pentecost—that was after I had gone up to heaven again—they did not quite understand it. Then they understood that by saying what I had said and doing what I had done they could bring me, my own self, down among them, and give me as food to feed the souls of everyone who loved me. I said first " my body " and then " my blood " instead of just " me ", because they were to remember my death when they did it. When anyone's body is separated from their blood that makes you think of their being dead, doesn't it? But they understood, and so do you, that I have gone back to heaven and that I am alive, not dead. So wherever my body or blood are, there am I. So when the priest gives you what looks like a little flat piece of bread in Holy Communion, that is really and truly me, myself, come to visit you, just as really and truly as I came to see the children in Nazareth. This is the very closest way I could possibly be with you: I live in your soul all the time if you are good, and in Holy Communion I come right into your body, too, to make you holy all through, body and soul as well.

You see, I made those special friends of mine able to pass on the power to bring me down among them. And it has been passed on ever since. The priest who says Mass for you has it, and so will other priests, right on to the end of the world.

Come to Holy Communion as often as you can, won't you ? If you do, you will find being good easier and easier and you will be happier and happier inside yourself, no matter what else happens to you. And you will find that that is the best time of all to talk to me and tell me all about what is being difficult for you, and what you would like me to do for you and for all your friends.

NINETEENTH CONVERSATION :

ABOUT TRUSTING GOD

Jesus: This is the last written-down conversation I am going to have with you just now, but you will not forget to talk to me because of that, will you ? I like so much to come and talk to you and hear what you have to tell me, and so few people ever bother to invite me. It is good to say prayers that you know by heart, of course, but if we are really friends I am sure you will want to talk to me besides saying those. And don't forget that I am always ready to listen, whenever you happen to think of it.

Now I am going to tell you a story!

Once upon a time, long before I came to live at Nazareth, there lived in the country

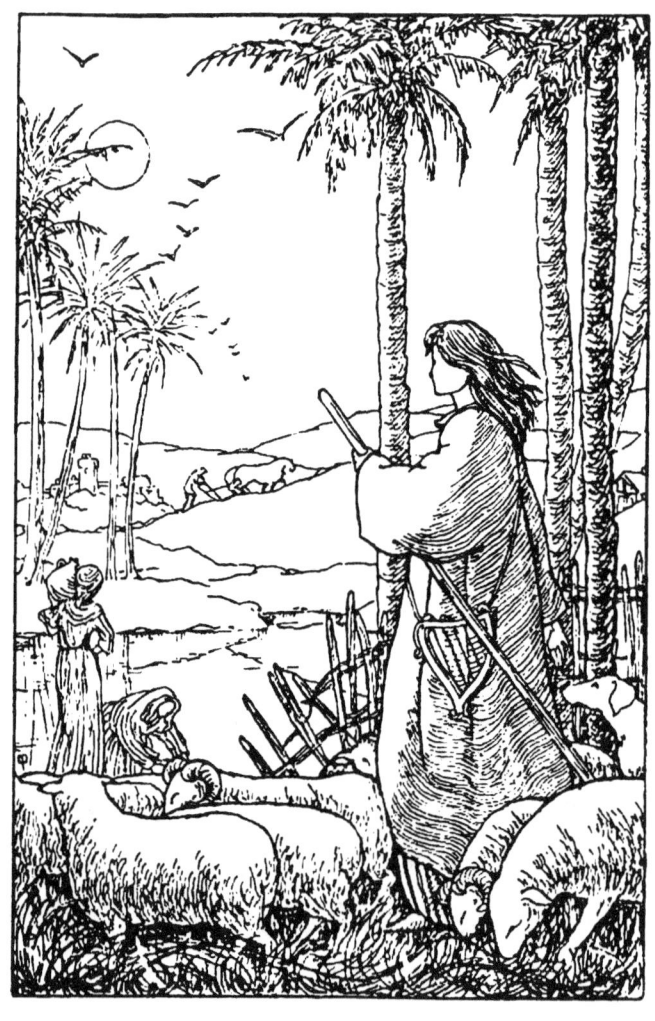

David

where I was to be born, a shepherd boy. His name was David, and he looked after his father's sheep all by himself up in the hills, where there was good grass for them.

At that time my country was at war with some very fierce people called the Philistines. David's big brothers had gone off to fight as soldiers, but David was too young to be in the army. He was a good-looking boy, with red hair, and a great friend of mine—he had plenty of time to talk to me, while the sheep wandered about eating grass. One day his father said to him, " Listen, David, I am going to give you a parcel of special cheeses and things to take to your brothers. You can see at the same time how they are getting on and bring me all the news."

David was delighted to be going off to see his brothers and the army and everything. He got up early next morning, put the big parcel in a bag slung over his shoulder, took his staff and went off whistling.

He had a long journey to find his brothers, and when he did find them they were glad to see him and the cheeses, but not at all cheerful otherwise. In fact the whole army was discouraged and worried. They told him that the Philistines had in their army a great fierce giant called Goliath and they were all afraid of him. He was so big no one else could have worn his heavy armour, and the soldier who had to carry his shield could scarcely manage to hold it up. Every morning he used to come out in front of the army and ask if there was anyone who would like to fight him, but they were all too frightened to say a word. So he used to laugh like anything and go back till next day.

" But that's dreadful! " said David. " If I had a chance I would go out and kill him."

At first his brothers laughed at him, but when they saw he really meant it they got cross and said, " You are nothing but a naughty, disobedient boy—I don't believe Father sent you here at all—you just came on your own, because you wanted to see the soldiers! Go home and look after the sheep! "

But David didn't go home. He went to look for the king, who was being a general, too, and was with the army. His name was Saul; and if the soldiers were worried about what was going on, you can imagine he was even more worried than they were. When David found him he said, " If you would only let me, I would go and kill this silly giant for you."

King Saul was too polite to laugh out loud, but he said, " You forget that you are only a boy, and this giant, besides being extra big and fierce, has been fighting all his life. What do you think you could do against him? "

" But I am a shepherd," said David, " and I look after my father's sheep, all by myself. I have killed a lion that came to steal a sheep before now, and a bear, too. Do you think that God, who saved me from being torn to pieces by a lion and a bear, couldn't keep me safe if I was fighting this wicked Philistine? "

King Saul was very much surprised at that, and at last he said, " Go and fight him then, and the Lord be with you."

He wanted David to wear his armour and his helmet and sword, but when David put them on they were so heavy and so much too big for him he could hardly move.

" I couldn't possibly fight anybody like this," he said, and he put on his ordinary everyday shepherd's clothes again. Then he went down to a stream and chose some small, sharp stones, and went out to meet the giant alone with his staff and his sling for weapons. A sling is a thing for throwing stones, something like a catapult.

When the giant Goliath saw him coming he laughed and laughed, and at the sound of his laughter the whole army who were watching David were more frightened than ever.

" Do you think I am a dog," he shouted, " to be frightened by a stick ? Come here and I will kill you and give you to the wolves to eat for their dinner."

David shouted back, " You think I ought to be afraid of your lance and sword, but I am coming against you in the name of God, whom you have insulted!"

Saying this, he took a stone out of his bag and threw it with his sling. It hit the giant in the middle of his forehead, and he fell down with such a crash the earth shook. The army behind David began to cheer and the Philistines to cry out in fright, but David didn't stop to listen to either of them. He ran up to the giant, took the great sword out of his hand and ran it through his heart.

Then he cut his great head off and carried it back to King Saul.

For a reward, when he grew up, he married the Princess Michol, the king's daughter, and he became a great king himself. And it was into his family that I came, when I was born on earth, hundreds of years later.

Now you will hear it said again and again as you grow up that there is a great deal of wickedness in the world, and that for you to try and fight against it is silly—you are too young, the wickedness has been going on for too long, it is far too strong for *you* to fight against, and so on. When you hear such things, just remember David and Goliath. However strong wickedness is, it is never a good plan to make friends with it, or to be frightened of it. Because nothing is so strong as me. So long as you stay on my side, even if you are killed, you will still win. If you do not remember that, and agree to be wicked, too, for the sake of being like everyone else, or getting something you want, or for any reason at all, then, however good a time you have in this world, you are bound to lose in the end. In the end it is always my friends who win, and the friends of the Devil who lose.

So trust me always, never forget what a powerful friend you have, never be discouraged if wicked people seem to get the best of it in this world. Let us grow up together, and come to heaven with me at last, where I have a special place waiting just for you, and such joy as you cannot even imagine, planned to be yours for ever and ever and ever.

A WORD FROM THE AUTHOR

THIS is really a book of beginnings of conversations you might have with Jesus. None of them says all the things you will want to talk to him about, or all the things he will want to say to you. They are just meant to start you off. You will find it is quite easy to go on telling him about all sorts of things, and that he is always ready to listen, any time at all.

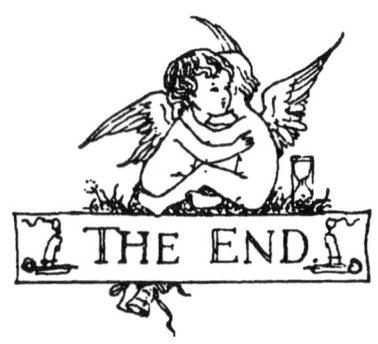

THE END.

www.ingramcontent.com/pod-product-compliance
Lightning Source LLC
Chambersburg PA
CBHW051344170526
45166CB00002B/944